OVERCOME YOUR FEAR OF
PUBLIC SPEAKING

LISA KLEIMAN

OVERCOME YOUR FEAR OF PUBLIC SPEAKING

PRACTICE DAILY EXERCISES AND JOURNAL

speaktopia.com

CONTENTS

COURAGE

OVERVIEW

INTRODUCTION

LET'S GET STARTED!

DAILY EXERCISES AND JOURNAL

1 — Understand Your Fear
13

2 — Build Confidence
43

3 — Refine Your Skills
73

4 — Integration and Mastery
103

YOU DID IT!

ADDITIONAL TRAINING
145

Copyright © 2024 by Lisa Kleiman

All rights reserved. No part of this book may be reproduced in any manner whatsoever without written permission except in the case of brief quotations embodied in critical articles and reviews.

First Printing, 2024

COURAGE

"Courage isn't the absence of fear, but the triumph over it. Every step toward becoming a confident speaker is a testament to your bravery – embracing vulnerability, overcoming doubts, and unleashing your voice."

NELSON MANDELA

OVERVIEW

Congratulations! You are addressing what many people avoid – facing their fear of public speaking. Many people won't and don't want to get started on becoming a confident speaker because they are afraid of the process.

Research shows that up to 74% of people experience some form of speech anxiety, also known as A FEAR OF PUBLIC SPEAKING.

Some people are so afraid of public speaking that they'll avoid it at all costs and allow their fear to limit their possibilities, negatively affecting their careers and relationships.

However, learning any skill, whether playing an instrument or a sport, takes effort and steps—and yes, it's a process.

This workbook can help you with the process of becoming a confident speaker.

It is designed to guide you step by step. You won't be asked to do monumental exercises such as getting up on stage in front of many people to give a speech – until you are ready.

Each exercise is meant to nudge you, gently push you outside of your comfort zone, and challenge you to overcome the limiting hurdles of each aspect of progress.

You may be curious about how this book can help you and, more importantly, what will be expected of you.

These FAQs may help.

1. Is this program expensive? Will I need to buy anything to complete the daily exercises?

NO! All exercises are free. You won't need to spend money on anything to complete the daily challenge exercises.

2. How much time is required to complete each daily challenge?

Each challenge should take 15 - 30 minutes of focused time, but that depends on you. You'll benefit from any amount of time you put into it.

3. Can I skip any of the exercises?

Well, yes—this workbook is for you to do as you want. However, we encourage you to do all the exercises in consecutive order to maximize your skill-building. The program is designed to guide you in building a foundation for growth.

4. Can I do the exercises from home and work?

Yes, you can do the exercises anywhere – at work, at home, in a hotel, in the car, with a friend, colleague, or loved one. You could also involve others and let them join the fun –supporting each other's speaking journey.

5. I don't have much formal presentation experience; will this program apply to me?

Of course! This program is designed to help anyone become a confident speaker regardless of their experience and expertise with public speaking.

6. I would like to get additional speaking practice. What are my options?

We applaud your efforts beyond this program to improve your speaking skills! This book includes instructions on how to practice as you develop your confidence. Other options include volunteering to speak at community events, at work, at schools, and Toastmasters, to name a few. At this time of this writing, Speaktopia offers ongoing "Practice Circle" online sessions where experienced facilitators lead participants to practice speaking in a supportive group. More details at www.speaktopia.com

Becoming a confident speaker may involve overcoming obstacles and facing fears, but the rewards of improved confidence and communication skills are well worth the effort.

This workbook is designed to help you become a more confident and effective speaker.

Here's what you can expect from this program:

Increased Confidence: As you progress through the daily exercises and face your fear of public speaking head-on, you'll experience a boost in confidence. You'll learn to trust your abilities and communicate confidently on and off the stage.

Improved Communication Skills: Through consistent practice and feedback, you'll refine your communication skills, including articulation, vocal delivery, and body language. You'll become adept at conveying your ideas clearly and persuasively, making you a more effective communicator in any setting.

Enhanced Leadership Abilities: Confidence in public speaking is often synonymous with effective leadership. By mastering the art of speaking with poise and authority, you'll naturally command respect and inspire others to act. Whether leading a team meeting or delivering a keynote address, your newfound confidence will elevate your leadership presence.

Expanded Career Opportunities: The ability to speak confidently in public opens doors to many career opportunities. Confident speakers are sought after across industries, whether delivering presentations, pitching ideas, or networking at events. You'll position yourself for career advancement and success by honing your speaking skills.

Building Meaningful Connections: Effective communication is the cornerstone of building meaningful connections. By mastering the art of public speaking, you'll foster stronger relationships, whether it's with colleagues, clients, or community members. Your ability to engage and inspire others will leave a lasting impression and build deeper connections.

Overcoming Fear and Anxiety: One of the most significant benefits of this program is overcoming the fear and anxiety associated with public speaking. As you confront your fears and develop strategies to manage them, you'll experience a sense of liberation and empowerment. Public speaking will no longer be a source of dread but an opportunity for growth and self-expression.

Personal Growth and Development: Beyond the tangible benefits, this program offers personal growth and development opportunities. As you push past your comfort zone, tackle challenges, and celebrate successes, you'll cultivate resilience, self-awareness, and a growth mindset. These qualities will serve you well in all areas of your life, far beyond public speaking.

Approach each challenge with an open mind and willingness to learn and grow.

INTRODUCTION

Let's nip your skepticism in the bud. You might think, "Will this 30-day program *REALLY* help me feel more confident as a speaker?" Perhaps you've tried other methods of overcoming your fear of public speaking through coursework, workshops, webinars, and coaching. But nothing worked well. Despite your attempts, you still feel anxious, experiencing the annoying and uncomfortable nerves that typically appear right before and when presenting and networking.

We won't promise that this book will be your holy grail and fix all your speaking issues. However, we firmly believe that the key to improving your public speaking skills lies in consistent effort and a shift in mindset. This book focuses on both.

Getting at the root of the fear of public speaking is perhaps the most effective method to speaking confidently for any speaking event because it addresses the issue at its core rather than simply treating the symptoms. By understanding and addressing the underlying causes of fear, individuals can develop long-lasting strategies to manage and overcome their anxiety, leading to genuine confidence and improved speaking abilities.

By committing to implementing all exercises with intention, taking the time to reflect, and incorporating them into your daily routine, you will gradually notice a reduction in overall anxiety and a significant boost in confidence when speaking in public.

Research in psychology and communication consistently supports the effectiveness of addressing the root causes of fear of public speaking for developing genuine confidence and speaking skills.

Cognitive-behavioral therapy (CBT) treats anxiety disorders, including social anxiety related to public speaking. Studies have shown that CBT techniques, such as cognitive restructuring (challenging and changing negative thought patterns) and exposure therapy (gradual exposure to feared situations), can significantly reduce public speaking anxiety and improve speaking confidence over time.

Self-efficacy, a concept developed by psychologist Albert Bandura, is about believing you can do things well. People who believe in themselves when speaking in public are more likely to feel confident and keep trying even when things get tough. You can boost your confidence in public speaking by facing your fears and improving through practice. Mindfulness helps people focus on the present moment without judging themselves. It's been found to help with public speaking anxiety. Research suggests that mindfulness practices such as deep breathing and meditation can calm the body and mind, making people feel more confident when speaking in front of others.

Research also shows positive psychology, such as focusing on strengths and reframing negative beliefs into positive thoughts, helps people develop confidence and resilience in speaking situations.

This 30-day confident speaking program incorporates all this. You'll discover your fears and then be guided daily with exercises that help you face and manage your fears and improve with practice.

LET'S GET STARTED!

Welcome to the **Overcome Your Fear of Public Speaking** program! Your 30-Day Guide to Speaking Success.

This program is designed to help you conquer your fear of public speaking by gradually exposing you to speaking situations, reframing negative thoughts, and building confidence through practice and reflection. Each day presents a new challenge, exercise, and space for documenting your experiences and key takeaways.

You only need to spend a few minutes each day on each exercise to notice improvement. However, take as long as you need for each exercise and go at your own pace. Rushing through the exercises doesn't serve anyone justice.

Remember—this is YOUR challenge. Do what you can and repeat any exercise if needed. Your effort to feel more confident in public speaking will benefit you.

For optimal results, complete your daily exercises consecutively, without missing a day, for 30 days.

And most importantly – have fun with this! Enjoy the process!

DAILY EXERCISES AND JOURNAL

UNDERSTAND YOUR FEAR

LISA KLEIMAN

DAY 1

ACKNOWLEDGE THE GOOD AND THE FEAR

Challenge

Reflecting on what specifically triggers your anxiety about public speaking is crucial for overcoming this common fear. Are you afraid of judgment, making mistakes, or blanking out during your speech? Pinpointing these concerns is the first step towards conquering them. Equally important is reflecting on past speaking engagements where you felt confident and received positive feedback. This can provide valuable insights and boost your confidence.

Exercises

Describe Your Fears

Write in detail about your fears and worries related to public speaking. Focus on specific scenarios or thoughts that provoke anxiety. Be as specific as possible in describing what aspects of public speaking make you anxious. This will help you gain clarity on the root causes of your apprehensions.

- **Example**: "I fear blanking out in the middle of my speech because I worry that the audience will think I'm unprepared and unprofessional."

Recall a Positive Experience

Describe a specific event where the audience responded well to your message. Include details about the setting, audience reaction, and your emotions before, during, and after the speech. Reflect on what factors contributed to your confidence and success during that speaking engagement. Consider aspects such as preparation, delivery, audience engagement, and the content of your message.

- **Example**: "Last year, I presented at a team meeting. The audience was engaged, nodded along, and asked questions afterward. I felt confident because I had practiced thoroughly and knew the material well."

Speaking Exercise: Two-Minute Self-Introduction

Record a two-minute video introducing yourself, explaining your interests, and why you want to improve your public speaking skills. Focus on being clear and concise. This exercise will help you get used to speaking about yourself and your goals, serving as a foundation for further public speaking practice.

When recording your first speech, don't worry about perfection or format. Simply speak into the recording device to get comfortable talking about your thoughts out loud. The goal is to ease into the process of verbal expression without the pressure of delivering a flawless performance.

Notes and Reflection

After completing both challenges and exercises, reflect on your findings and experiences. What insights did you gain from identifying your anxiety triggers and recalling past successful speaking engagements? Did you notice any patterns or commonalities in your fears and worries about public speaking? How do these compare to the factors that contributed to your success in past engagements? How can you leverage the insights gained to improve your confidence and performance in future speaking opportunities?

LISA KLEIMAN

DAY 2

Recognize Your Strengths

Challenge

Shift your focus from perceived weaknesses to strengths as a speaker, recognizing and embracing what you bring.

This challenge focuses on recognizing and harnessing your existing speaking strengths. By identifying your strengths, you can become an effective and confident speaker. This challenge involves exercises designed to help you uncover and leverage your unique strengths in public speaking.

Exercises

List Your Strengths

Identify your strengths as a speaker (e.g., storytelling ability, passion for your topic, charisma). Reflect on past speaking experiences where you demonstrated these strengths.

- **Example**: "I am good at storytelling and making complex topics interesting. I used a personal story to illustrate a key point during my last presentation, and the audience appeared engaged."

Collect Feedback

Ask friends, colleagues, or mentors for feedback on your speaking abilities. Compile their responses and compare them with your self-assessment.

- **Example**: Ask a colleague, "Can you tell me what you think are my strengths when I present?"

Speaking Exercise: Strength Highlight Speech

Prepare a short speech (3-5 minutes) highlighting one of your strengths. Deliver the speech with a focus on showcasing this strength. If your strength is storytelling, prepare a speech that includes a personal story to engage your audience. For example, share a memorable experience that taught you a valuable lesson, emphasizing how you craft the narrative to keep the audience interested.

- **Record Yourself**: Use a smartphone or camera to record your speech. Pay attention to how you incorporate your strengths throughout the delivery.
- **Assess Your Recording:** After recording, watch your speech and evaluate your performance based on the following criteria:
  - **Application of Strength**: Did you effectively showcase your chosen strength throughout the speech? Reflect on specific moments where this strength was most evident.
  - **Confidence and Presence**: Did you appear confident and in control? How was your overall presence on camera?
  - **Strength Application**: How effectively did you showcase your storytelling ability (or other strength)? Identify specific instances where this strength was most apparent and impactful.

- **Observations**: Note areas where you felt particularly strong or noticed room for improvement.

Notes and Reflection

After self-evaluating, take notes on your observations. Reflect on how effectively you used your strengths and identify any areas for improvement. Consider what you did well and what adjustments you can make to enhance your performance for future speeches.

LISA KLEIMAN

DAY 3

Analyze Fear Patterns

Challenge

Reflect on recurring patterns or themes in your fear of public speaking to gain insight into underlying causes and develop strategies to address them.

Exercises

Review Fear Triggers

Review your notes from Day 1 about your previous fear triggers and speaking experiences to identify common themes or patterns.

- **Template**:
    - Fear Trigger: _____
    - Common Theme/Pattern: _____
    - Specific Example: _____
- **Example**:
    - Fear Trigger: Speaking without preparation
    - Common Theme/Pattern: Fear of judgment
    - Specific Example: "I often feel anxious when speaking without preparation because I worry that the audience might judge me harshly."

Explore Underlying Causes

Consider factors such as past traumas, negative beliefs, or social conditioning that may contribute to your fear. Explore how these patterns manifest in your thoughts, emotions, and physical sensations.

- **Template**:
    - Underlying Cause: _____
    - Manifestation: _____
    - Specific Example: _____
- **Example**:
    - Underlying Cause: Past negative experience
    - Manifestation: Fear of forgetting material, anxiety
    - Specific Example: "I realized that my fear of public speaking started after a bad experience in school where I forgot my lines during a play. This has made me fear forgetting my material in front of an audience."

Speaking Exercise: Impromptu Speech on Fear Patterns

Choose a random topic and speak about it for 2-3 minutes without preparation. Record yourself and observe how you handle spontaneous speaking situations. Focus on identifying any anxiety triggers and managing them during the speech.

- **Example**: Speak about "the importance of exercise" without any preparation. Pay attention to moments of anxiety and how you cope with them.

Self-Evaluation

After recording, watch your speech and evaluate your performance based on the following criteria:

- **Identification of Fear Patterns**: Did you notice recurring themes or triggers during your impromptu speech?

- **Handling of Anxiety**: How did you manage moments of anxiety or fear during the speech?
- **Application of Insights**: Were you able to apply any strategies to manage your fear based on the patterns and causes you've identified?

Self-Evaluation Template

- **Fear Patterns Identified**: _____
- **Handling of Anxiety**: _____
- **Application of Insights**: _____

Notes and Reflection

Reflect on your observations and experiences:

- **Patterns and Triggers**: What specific patterns or triggers did you identify?

- **Strategies for Management**: How can you use these insights to develop strategies for managing your fear in future speaking situations?

- **Reflection Example**: "During the impromptu speech, I noticed I felt most anxious at the beginning. My heart started racing, so I stopped speaking and tried again. I tried smiling and laughing at myself, which seemed to help. I will practice this technique in future speeches."

LISA KLEIMAN

DAY 4

Challenge Negative Beliefs

Challenge

In Day 3, you analyzed recurring patterns and underlying causes of your fear of public speaking. Today's challenge focuses on addressing those fears by challenging negative beliefs and replacing them with positive affirmations. This exercise is crucial for transforming the insights gained in previous exercises into actionable strategies for overcoming fear.

Exercises

Identify Negative Thoughts

Identify a negative thought or belief you have about public speaking. Be specific and honest with yourself about these thoughts.

- **Example**: "I often think, 'I'm not a good speaker,' which makes me feel nervous and unprepared."
- **Template**:
    - Negative Thought/Belief: _____

Challenge and Reframe

Write down evidence contradicting this negative thought and reframe it into a more positive or empowering statement.

- **Example**: "I've successfully given presentations before and received positive feedback. I am capable and confident."

- **Template:**
    - Negative Thought/Belief: _____
    - Contradicting Evidence: _____
    - Positive Reframe: _____

Speaking Exercise: Affirmation Speech

Create a 3-minute speech using positive affirmations about your speaking abilities. Record yourself delivering the speech, focusing on embodying confidence and positivity. This speech should be recorded alone, without an audience, to help you concentrate on internalizing these positive affirmations.

- **Example**: "I am a confident and engaging speaker. I have valuable insights to share, and my audience is interested in what I say."
- **Template:**
    - Positive Affirmation: _____
    - Speech Content: _____

How to Review the Recording

When reviewing your recording, consider your tone, body language, and overall confidence. Evaluate how well you embody the positive affirmations.

- **Criteria:**
    - **Clarity and Articulation**: Did you speak clearly and confidently?
    - **Body Language**: Did your body language reflect confidence?
    - **Tone and Positivity**: Did your tone convey positivity and assurance?
- **Self-Evaluation Template:**
    - Clarity and Articulation: _____

- Body Language: _____
- Tone and Positivity: _____

Notes and Reflection

Document your experience reframing negative thoughts and delivering the affirmation speech. Note any shifts in perspective or feelings of empowerment. Reflect on how adopting a more positive mindset can impact your approach to public speaking.

Reflection Questions

- **What Negative Beliefs Were Challenged?**
- **How Did Reframing Affect Your Confidence?**
- **Impact on Future Public Speaking**: How can this positive mindset shift help you in future public speaking engagements?

LISA KLEIMAN

DAY 5

Understand Real Versus Improbable

Challenge

On Day 3, you identified recurring patterns and underlying causes of your fear of public speaking. On Day 4, you began challenging and reframing these negative beliefs. Today's exercises build on those insights by helping you critically evaluate the realism of your fears and separate fact from fiction. This will further empower you to address your anxiety with practical strategies.

Exercises

Evaluate Consequences

Describe the potential consequences you fear from public speaking. Evaluate if these fears are based on evidence or assumptions.

- **Template**:
    - Fear: _____
    - Potential Consequence: _____
    - Evidence or Assumption: _____
- **Example**:
    - Fear: "I will forget my speech, and everyone will laugh at me."
    - Potential Consequence: "Embarrassment and judgment."
    - Evidence or Assumption: "This has never happened, and my colleagues are generally supportive."

Upcoming Event Anxiety

If you have an upcoming speaking event, answer the following:

- What are you worried will happen?
- What are the consequences if this happens?
- How bad are the consequences?
- How likely is the consequence to happen?
- What is worse – the consequence of your speech or not doing the speech/speaking event?
- **Template**:
    - Worried Outcome: _____
    - Consequences: _____
    - Severity: _____
    - Likelihood: _____
    - Comparison: _____
- **Example**:
    - Worried Outcome: "I will forget my points."
    - Consequences: "I might feel embarrassed."
    - Severity: "The consequences are not severe; I can use notes or prompts."
    - Likelihood: "The likelihood is low since I have practiced well."
    - Comparison: "Not doing the speech would be worse as it would hinder my growth and opportunities."

Speaking Exercise: Q&A Session

Prepare a brief talk on a familiar topic and invite a friend or family member to ask you questions afterward. Record the session and focus on how you manage the Q&A part, addressing any fears of unexpected questions.

- **Example**: Talk about your favorite hobby and handle related questions.
- **Template**:
    - Topic: _____
    - Questions: _____
    - Responses: _____

Alternative Exercise: Self-Q&A Session

Prepare a brief talk on a familiar topic and write down a list of potential questions you think an audience might ask. Record yourself asking and then answering these questions, simulating a Q&A session.

- **Example**: Talk about your favorite hobby and write down questions like "Why did you choose this hobby?" and "What do you enjoy most?" Then, record yourself answering these questions.
- **Template**:
    - Topic: _____
    - Questions: _____
    - Responses: _____

How to Review the Recording

When reviewing your recording, consider how you handle unexpected questions, your confidence levels, and your ability to stay calm.

- **Criteria**:
    - **Handling Unexpected Questions**: Were you able to respond clearly and confidently?
    - **Calmness and Composure**: Did you remain calm and composed during the Q&A?

- **Use of Strategies**: Did you use any strategies to manage anxiety during the session?
- **Self-Evaluation Template**:
    - Handling Unexpected Questions:
    - Calmness and Composure:
    - Use of Strategies:

Notes and Reflection

Reflect on the insights you discovered about the truths of what you fear and how you managed the Q&A session. Consider how you can benefit from this exercise whenever you feel anxious about an upcoming speaking event.

Reflection Questions

- **Real vs. Improbable Fears**: What insights did you discover about the truths of what you fear?

- **Managing Anxiety**: How did you manage your anxiety during the Q&A session?

- **Future Strategies**: How could you benefit from doing this exercise regularly to prepare for speaking events?

DAY 6

Visualize Your Preferred Outcome

Challenge

In Day 3, you identified the patterns and underlying causes of your fear. On Day 4, you challenged and reframed negative beliefs. Day 5 involved evaluating the realism of your fears. Today's exercise builds on these foundations by using visualization to create a positive mental image of public speaking, further solidifying a confident and successful mindset.

Exercises
Visualization Exercise

Visualize an event in your past that made you feel inadequate, anxious, and perhaps fearful when speaking in public. Answer the following questions as you visualize:

- What happened?
- How did you feel?
- What were the consequences?
- How did this affect your confidence?
- Then, visualize how you wish it would have happened. Include specific details such as:
    - **Colors**: What colors do you see? Describe the environment and any visuals.
    - **Sounds**: What sounds are present? Is there background noise, applause, or silence?

- **Emotions**: What emotions are you feeling? Focus on positive emotions like confidence and happiness.
- **Smells**: Are there any particular smells that stand out?
- **Reactions of Others**: How is the audience reacting? Are they smiling, nodding, or clapping?
- **Objects**: What objects are around you? Describe the setting, such as a podium, microphone, or presentation materials.
- **Example**:
  - **Negative Event**: "I once felt very nervous during a presentation and stumbled over my words."
  - **Feelings**: "I felt embarrassed and lost confidence."
  - **Consequences**: "I hesitated to volunteer for speaking opportunities afterward."
  - **Visualization**:
    - **Colors**: "The room is brightly lit with soft, warm colors that make me feel comfortable."
    - **Sounds**: "I hear light background music that calms me, followed by the gentle hum of attentive listeners."
    - **Emotions**: "I feel a wave of confidence and calmness as I begin to speak."
    - **Smells**: "There is a faint smell of coffee from the refreshment table, adding to the cozy atmosphere."
    - **Others' Reactions**: "The audience is smiling, nodding in agreement, and clapping at key points."
    - **Objects**: "I see my presentation slides on the screen, a microphone in my hand, and my notes on the podium."

- **Outcome**: "I see myself speaking clearly and confidently, with the audience engaged and responsive. I feel a sense of accomplishment afterward."

Speaking Exercise: Positive Visualization Speech

Create a speech in which you describe the positive visualization in detail. Record yourself and focus on expressing the confidence and success you imagined.

Example: Describe your visualization of a successful presentation, including the audience's positive reactions and your confidence.

Template:

- **Introduction**: Briefly describe the past negative event.
- **Visualization Details**: Explain how you visualize the event differently, focusing on positive outcomes.
- **Conclusion**: Reflect on the feelings of confidence and success from the visualization.

How to Review the Recording

Remember how vividly and confidently you describe the positive visualization when reviewing your recording.

Criteria:

- **Clarity and Detail**: Did you clearly describe the visualization with detailed sensory information (colors, sounds, emotions, smells, reactions of others, objects)?
- **Confidence and Positivity**: Did you express confidence and positivity in your tone and body language?

- **Engagement**: Did you engage with the visualization as if it were a real, positive experience?

Self-Evaluation Template:

- Clarity and Detail: _____
- Confidence and Positivity: _____
- Engagement: _____

Notes and Reflection

After completing the exercise, evaluate how you feel about the event. Reflect on the power of visualization in changing your perception and confidence in public speaking.

Reflection Questions

- **Feelings After Visualization**: How do you feel about the event after visualizing a positive outcome?

- **Impact of Visualization**: How has the visualization exercise affected your perception and confidence in public speaking?

DAY 7

Set Realistic Goals

Challenge

In the first week, you have identified patterns of fear, challenged negative beliefs, and used visualization to enhance confidence. Today's exercise builds on these foundations by setting specific, actionable goals. Creating goals at the end of Week 1 is valuable as it helps you consolidate your learnings and provides a clear roadmap for the remaining 30 days of the challenge program.

Exercises

Identify Areas for Improvement

Identify areas of your public speaking skills that you want to improve. Clearly define what you want to achieve. For example, instead of a vague goal like "overcome my fear of public speaking," set a specific goal such as "deliver a five-minute presentation without forgetting my speech due to nervousness."

- **Template:**
    - Area for Improvement: _____
    - Specific Goal: _____
- **Example:**
    - Area for Improvement: "Memory and managing nervousness."

- Specific Goal: "I want to deliver a five-minute presentation without forgetting my speech due to nervousness."

Action Plan

Create a detailed action plan to achieve your goals. Break down the steps you need to take and set deadlines for each step.

- **Template:**
    - Goal: _____
    - Steps to Achieve Goal:
        1. __
        2. __
        3. __
    - Deadlines: _____
- **Example:**
    - Goal: "Deliver a five-minute presentation without forgetting my speech due to nervousness."
    - Steps to Achieve Goal:
        1. Diligently complete each remaining day's exercise in the 30-day challenge program.
        2. Apply relaxation and visualization techniques provided in the exercises to manage anxiety and boost confidence.
        3. Use each day's feedback opportunities to get input from friends, family, or mentors and incorporate their suggestions.
        4. Self-assess and reflect on each day's practice and improvements, noting what worked well and needs adjustment.

Speaking Exercise: Goal Setting Speech

Deliver a speech outlining your goals and action plan for improving your public speaking skills. Record yourself and focus on articulating your goals clearly and confidently.

- **Template**:
    - **Introduction**: Briefly introduce the importance of setting realistic goals at the end of Week 1.
    - **Goals**: Clearly outline your specific goals.
    - **Action Plan**: Detail the steps you will take to achieve these goals.
    - **Conclusion**: Reflect on how these goals will help you improve and stay motivated throughout the 30-day challenge.
- **Example**:
    - **Introduction**: "Setting realistic goals at the end of Week 1 is crucial for building on what we've learned and staying motivated."
    - **Goals**: "My specific goal is to deliver a five-minute presentation without forgetting my speech due to nervousness."
    - **Action Plan**: "To achieve this, I will practice my speech twice daily, record and review my performance, incorporate relaxation techniques, seek feedback, and gradually increase speech length."
    - **Conclusion**: "Following this plan will build my confidence and become a more effective speaker, setting the stage for success over the next 30 days."

How to Review the Recording

When reviewing your recording, consider how clearly you articulate your goals and how confident you appear.

- **Criteria**:

- **Clarity and Specificity**: Did you clearly and specifically state your goals?
- **Confidence**: Did you appear confident and motivated while outlining your plan?
- **Engagement**: Did you engage with the goals as meaningful and achievable?
- **Self-Evaluation Template**:
  - Clarity and Specificity: _____
  - Confidence: _____
  - Engagement: _____

Notes and Reflection

Document your goals and action plan for improving your public speaking skills. Reflect on how setting realistic goals can help you stay motivated and focused on overcoming fear.

Reflection Questions

- **Documented Goals and Action Plan**: What specific goals and action plans have you documented?

- **Motivation and Focus**: How has setting realistic goals helped you stay motivated and focused on your public speaking improvement?

- **Future Steps**: How can you continue building on these goals?

BUILD CONFIDENCE

LISA KLEIMAN

DAY 8

Practice Relaxation Techniques

Challenge

Over the past week, you've worked on understanding your fears, setting goals, and visualizing positive outcomes. These steps have laid the foundation for identifying when and why you feel anxious about public speaking. Today's exercises focus on practical methods to manage and mitigate that anxiety, ensuring you can effectively implement your plans and visualizations.

The challenge today is to apply these relaxation techniques to reduce physiological symptoms of anxiety, such as increased heart rate and muscle tension, and to achieve mental calmness and focus.

Benefits of Relaxation Techniques

- **Physiological Benefits**: Relaxation techniques help lower heart rate, reduce muscle tension, and slow breathing, which counteracts the body's fight-or-flight response. This physiological calmness can prevent the symptoms of anxiety that interfere with clear thinking and confident speaking.
- **Mental Benefits**: These techniques promote mindfulness and present-moment awareness, reducing racing thoughts and mental distractions. Focusing on the present can reduce worries about potential negative outcomes, enhancing your ability to stay composed and focused.

Exercises

Deep Breathing Exercise

Inhale deeply for a count of four, hold for four, and exhale slowly for a count of four. Repeat several times.

- **Example**: Sit comfortably, close your eyes, and practice this breathing technique until you feel more relaxed.

Progressive Muscle Relaxation

Tense and relax different muscle groups, starting from your toes and working your way up to your head.

- **Example**: Tense the muscles in your feet for five seconds, then relax them. Move up to your calves, thighs, abdomen, chest, arms, and head and neck.

Mindfulness Meditation

Practice mindfulness meditation to cultivate present-moment awareness and calm racing thoughts.

- **Example**: Sit quietly, focus on your breath, and gently bring your attention back to your breath whenever your mind starts to wander.

Smile and Breathe

Take a deep breath and smile as you exhale. Hold your smile through several repetitions.

- **Example**: Smile, take a deep breath in, and as you exhale, maintain your smile. Repeat this process several times.

Speaking Exercise: Relaxation-Guided Speech

Record a short speech in which you guide yourself (and potentially others) through one of the relaxation exercises you practiced. Focus on maintaining a calm and soothing tone.

- **Example**: Record a speech where you guide yourself through the deep breathing exercise, explaining each step as you go.

Notes and Reflection

Document your experience practicing relaxation techniques, noting any changes in your physical sensations or overall calmness. Identify which techniques resonate most with you for future use.

Reflection Questions

- **Physical Sensations**: What physical changes did you notice during and after practicing the relaxation techniques?

- **Overall Calmness**: How did your overall level of calmness change?

- **Preferred Techniques**: Which relaxation techniques resonated most with you, and why?

- **Future Use**: How can you incorporate these techniques before speaking engagements?

LISA KLEIMAN

DAY 9

Reframe Fear as Excitement

Challenge

In the first week, you identified and challenged your fears, set realistic goals, and practiced techniques to manage anxiety. Reframing fear as excitement takes this a step further by transforming your mental and emotional response to speaking, allowing you to harness nervous energy positively.

Reframe nervousness or fear as excitement and anticipation, channeling that energy into enthusiasm when speaking. This builds on relaxation techniques by transforming your mental and emotional response to public speaking.

Why and How Reframing Works

For reframing to be effective, you must understand and believe why and how it works. Reframing is powerful because it leverages the physiological similarity between fear and excitement. Both emotions trigger similar responses in the body, such as an increased heart rate and adrenaline rush. By consciously interpreting these physical signs as excitement rather than fear, you can channel that energy into a positive force that enhances your performance. To ensure this mindset shift is believable, incorporate reasons that resonate with you.

Exercises

Reframe Thoughts

Before speaking, remember nervousness is a natural response to excitement and anticipation. Shift your focus from the negative aspects of fear to the positive energy it can provide for your performance.

- **Example**: Tell yourself, "My nervousness is just excitement in disguise. I can use this energy to deliver a powerful speech."

Daily Reframing

Reframe any anxious thoughts throughout your day with positive statements that are believable and meaningful to you. Use statements like, "I am excited to share my message with the audience because I believe in its importance and value" or "I thrive on the adrenaline of public speaking because it sharpens my focus and enhances my delivery." Understanding and believing in the reasons behind your reframing statements is crucial for them to work effectively.

- **Example**: Before a meeting, tell yourself, "I am excited to contribute my ideas and engage with my colleagues because my perspective can make a difference."

Speaking Exercise: Excitement Speech

Record a speech describing a situation when you successfully reframed fear as excitement. Focus on how this mindset shift impacted your performance and energy levels.

- **Example**: Describe when you were nervous before a presentation but told yourself it was excitement because you believed the audience would benefit from the message, leading to an energetic and engaging delivery.

Notes and Reflection

Document your experience reframing fear as excitement before speaking, noting any changes in your mindset or energy level. Reflect on how shifting your perspective can transform fear into a source of motivation and empowerment.

Reflection Questions

- **Mindset Changes**: What changes did you notice in your mindset when you reframed fear as excitement?

- **Energy Levels**: How did this mindset shift affect your energy levels and overall performance?

- **Future Application**: How can you continue to use this technique to enhance your public speaking?

LISA KLEIMAN

DAY 10

Practice Self Compassion

Challenge

Cultivate self-compassion and kindness towards yourself as you navigate public speaking challenges. Building on reframing fear, this day nurtures a positive and supportive inner dialogue.

Exercises

Notice Self-Critical Thoughts

Notice any self-critical thoughts or judgments today. Write them down.

- **Example**: "I often think, 'I'm not good enough at public speaking.'"

Self-Compassionate Self-Talk

Practice self-compassionate self-talk by offering yourself words of encouragement and support (e.g., "It's okay to make mistakes," "I'm learning and growing with each experience").

- **Example**: Replace "I'm not good enough" with "I am improving with every practice session."

Treat Yourself with Kindness

Treat yourself with kindness and understanding, especially during moments of vulnerability or fear.

- **Example**: Take a break if you're overwhelmed, or reward yourself after a practice session.

Speaking Exercise: Self-Compassion Speech

Create and record a speech where you talk about the importance of self-compassion and how it can help you in public speaking. Share your insights.

- **Example**: "Practicing self-compassion has helped me be kinder and more resilient in the face of challenges. It reminds me that everyone makes mistakes and that growth comes from learning and trying again."

How to Review the Recording

When reviewing your recording, evaluate how well you conveyed the concept of self-compassion and its impact on your speaking confidence.

- **Criteria**:
    - **Clarity**: Did you clearly explain the importance of self-compassion?
    - **Sincerity**: Did you genuinely express self-compassion and its benefits?
    - **Impact**: Did you reflect on how self-compassion improved your public speaking?
- **Self-Evaluation Template**:
    - Clarity: _____
    - Sincerity: _____
    - Impact: _____

Notes and Reflection

Reflect on your experience of practicing self-compassion, noting any shifts in your attitude towards yourself and public speaking. Consider how self-compassion can enhance resilience and self-confidence in speaking situations.

LISA KLEIMAN

DAY 11

Practice Positive Affirmations

Challenge

Having practiced self-compassion, you are ready to reinforce those positive feelings with affirmations. By consistently using affirmations, you solidify the supportive inner dialogue cultivated through self-compassion, making it easier to maintain a confident mindset.

Harness the power of positive affirmations to reprogram your subconscious mind and boost confidence. This builds on self-compassion by reinforcing positive self-talk.

Importance of Believable Affirmations

- **Believability**: For affirmations to work, they must be realistic and truthful. If an affirmation feels false or exaggerated, your subconscious mind will reject it, undermining its effectiveness.
- **Reprogramming the Subconscious**: Believable affirmations help to reprogram your subconscious mind by replacing negative self-talk with positive, supportive statements. This shift can enhance your self-esteem and public speaking confidence over time.

Exercises

Create Affirmations

Create a list of positive, truthful, and realistic affirmations related to public speaking (e.g., "I am a confident and captivating speaker," "I have valuable insights to share").

· **Example**: "I am a confident and engaging speaker."

Daily Repetition

Repeat these affirmations aloud or in your mind throughout the day.

· **Example**: Repeat "I am confident and capable" multiple times daily, especially before speaking.

Challenge Negative Self-Talk

Notice any resistance or skepticism and challenge negative self-talk with affirmations.

· **Example**: If you think, "I can't do this," counter it with "I am prepared and capable."

Speaking Exercise: Affirmation Speech

Record a speech where you share positive affirmations and explain how they help boost confidence. Reflect on any shifts in your self-perception or mindset.

· **Example**: "Using affirmations like 'I am a confident speaker' has helped me change my mindset and feel more empowered."

How to Review the Recording

When reviewing your recording, assess the clarity and conviction with which you delivered your affirmations.

· **Criteria**:

- **Clarity**: Did you clearly state your affirmations?
 - **Conviction**: Did you deliver your affirmations with belief and confidence?
 - **Impact**: Did you reflect on the positive impact of affirmations on your mindset?
- **Self-Evaluation Template**:
 - Clarity: _____
 - Conviction: _____
 - Impact: _____

Notes and Reflection

Reflect on your experience of practicing positive affirmations, noting any shifts in your self-perception or mindset. Pay attention to how affirmations influence your confidence and performance in speaking situations.

LISA KLEIMAN

DAY 12

Embrace Authenticity

Challenge

You are ready to focus on authenticity after building confidence through relaxation techniques, reframing fear, and practicing self-compassion and positive affirmations. Authenticity in public speaking allows you to connect with your audience deeper, making your messages more impactful and memorable.

Embrace authenticity as a cornerstone of confident public speaking. Identify aspects of your authentic self that you want to bring into your speaking style, such as your personality, values, and unique perspective.

Exercises

Reflect on Authenticity

Reflect on your authentic self and what makes you unique as a speaker. Consider aspects of your personality, values, and experiences that you want to highlight. Ask yourself:

- What am I passionate about?
- What values are important to me?
- What personal experiences have shaped who I am?
- **Example**: "I am passionate about storytelling and connecting with my audience personally."

Identify Your Authentic Self

To know what your authentic self is, write down your core values, interests, and qualities. Think about how you interact with friends and family versus how you present yourself professionally. The goal is to align these versions of yourself.

- **Example**: "I value honesty and compassion. I enjoy making people laugh and feel understood. In my daily life, I am approachable and empathetic."

Speak Authentically

Convey your authenticity in your delivery by:

- **Being Honest**: Share your true thoughts and feelings.
- **Showing Compassion**: Use warm and inclusive language.
- **Using Personal Stories**: Incorporate personal anecdotes that illustrate your values.
- **Example**: If you are compassionate, show this by acknowledging your audience's emotions and using empathetic language. If you are honest, be straightforward and transparent in your communication.
    - **Example**: "I know many of you might be uncertain about this new project, and that's completely understandable. Change can be overwhelming."
    - **Examples Using Empathetic Language**: Use phrases that convey understanding and support.
        - "I hear you."
        - "It's okay to feel this way."
        - "We are all in this together."
        - "Your feelings are valid."
        - "Let's work through this challenge as a team."

Authentic Speech

Practice delivering a short speech or presentation that reflects your authentic voice and style. Focus on being genuine and heartfelt.

- **Example**: Share a personal story that highlights your values and experiences. "I want to share a story about overcoming a challenge in my life and how it shaped who I am today."

Speaking Exercise: Authentic Expression

Record a speech where you share a personal story or experience that reflects your true self. Focus on being genuine and heartfelt.

- **Example**: "I want to share a story about overcoming a challenge in my life and how it shaped who I am today."

Speaking Exercise (Solo Option)

Stand in front of a mirror and deliver your speech, observing your body language and facial expressions to ensure they match the authenticity of your message. Focus on speaking with warmth and empathy.

- **Example**: "I am going to share a story about a time when I felt overwhelmed and how I managed to get through it by relying on my values of honesty and compassion."

How to Review the Recording

When reviewing your recording, evaluate how authentically you presented yourself and connected with your audience.

- **Criteria**:
    - **Authenticity**: Did you genuinely express your true self?

- **Engagement**: Did your story engage and resonate with your audience?
- **Emotion**: Did you convey genuine emotions effectively?
- **Self-Evaluation Template**:
    - Authenticity: _____
    - Engagement: _____
    - Emotion: _____

Notes and Reflection

Reflect on your experience of embracing authenticity in your public speaking. How did it feel to speak from a place of authenticity and vulnerability? What feedback did you receive from others, and how did they respond to your authentic expression? How can you continue cultivating authenticity in your public speaking practice moving forward?

- **Reflection Questions**:
    - How did embracing your authentic self impact your confidence and connection with your audience?
    - What aspects of your authentic self were most effective in your speech?
    - How will you continue to integrate authenticity into your future public speaking engagements?

DAY 13

Develop a Pre-Speech Ritual

Challenge

Throughout the past few days, you have learned various techniques such as relaxation, positive affirmations, and embracing authenticity. A pre-speech ritual combines these elements into a cohesive routine that prepares you mentally and physically for public speaking.

Create a pre-speech ritual or routine to help you mentally prepare and enter a confident state before speaking. This challenge builds on previous exercises by establishing a consistent routine to reduce anxiety and enhance performance.

Exercises

Design a Routine

Design a pre-speech routine with calming activities such as deep breathing, visualization, or positive self-talk. Your routine should be short enough to perform before you speak but comprehensive enough to help you feel centered and confident.

- **Example Routine**:
  1. **Deep Breathing**: Inhale deeply for four counts, hold for four, and exhale for four. Repeat three times.
  2. **Visualization**: Visualize a successful speech where the audience is engaged and responsive.

3. **Positive Self-Talk**: Recite affirmations such as "I am prepared and confident. My message is valuable and will resonate with the audience."

Practice the Ritual

Practice your pre-speech ritual multiple times today before speaking in person, on the phone, or online. The more you practice, the more natural and effective the ritual will become.

Adjust and Refine

Adjust and refine your ritual based on what helps you feel most centered and focused. Experiment with different elements and durations to find the most effective combination.

- **Example**: If visualizing for one minute isn't enough, extend it to two minutes. If deep breathing feels too short, add a few more breaths.

Speaking Exercise: Ritual Sharing

Record a speech where you explain your pre-speech ritual and how it helps you prepare for speaking engagements. Share tips and insights for creating an effective ritual.

- **Example**: "My pre-speech ritual includes deep breathing, visualization, and positive affirmations. These steps help me feel calm and focused. Visualizing the audience's positive reactions boosts my confidence."

How to Review the Recording

When reviewing your recording, assess how clearly you explained your pre-speech ritual and its effectiveness.

- **Criteria**:
  - **Clarity**: Did you clearly explain each step of your ritual?
  - **Effectiveness**: Did you convey how the ritual helps you prepare for speaking?
  - **Practicality**: Did you provide practical tips for creating an effective ritual?
- **Self-Evaluation Template**:
  - Clarity: _____
  - Effectiveness: _____
  - Practicality: _____

Notes and Reflection

Document your experience developing and implementing a pre-speech ritual, noting any changes in your mindset or performance before speaking. Reflect on the effectiveness of your ritual and any adjustments you may want to make moving forward.

Reflection Questions

- How did the pre-speech ritual impact your confidence and performance?
- Which ritual elements were most effective in helping you feel centered and focused?
- What adjustments did you make to refine your ritual, and how did these changes affect your preparation and delivery?

LISA KLEIMAN

DAY 14

Visualize Your Audience's Support

Challenge

Building on relaxation techniques, positive affirmations, and authenticity, visualization leverages your mental imagery to create a positive and supportive environment in your mind. This practice helps solidify your confidence and prepares you to handle actual speaking engagements with more assurance.

Use visualization techniques to imagine yourself delivering a successful and confident speech. Visualization can help reduce anxiety and improve performance by mentally preparing you for a positive outcome.

Exercises

Choose a Speaking Opportunity

Choose an upcoming public speaking opportunity you feel nervous about, such as a presentation or meeting.

- **Example**: "I have a team meeting next week where I need to present a project update."

Visualization Exercise

Find a quiet space to relax and visualize the upcoming speaking opportunity in vivid detail.

- **Step-by-Step Visualization:**
  1. **Environment**: Picture the room where you will be speaking. Notice the colors, lighting, and arrangement of the space.
  2. **Audience**: Visualize your audience seated and ready to listen. Imagine their faces smiling, nodding, and showing engagement.
  3. **Yourself**: See yourself standing confidently, making eye contact, and using positive body language.
  4. **Details**: Focus on your posture, gestures, and how you move around the space.
  5. **Reactions**: Imagine the audience's positive reactions, such as nodding in agreement, smiling, and clapping.
  6. **Feedback**: Visualize receiving positive feedback and applause at the end of your presentation.
- **Example**: "I see myself standing confidently at the front of the room, making eye contact with my colleagues, and seeing them smile and nod in agreement. I feel calm and in control as I speak clearly and passionately about my project."

Speaking Exercise: Supportive Audience Speech

Record a speech where you describe your visualization experience, focusing on the positive energy and support you imagined from your audience.

- **Example**: "In my visualization, I imagined my team fully engaged and supportive. They were smiling and nodding as I spoke, which made me feel more confident. At the end of my presentation, I visualized them clapping and giving me positive feedback, which boosted my confidence."

How to Review the Recording

When reviewing your recording, evaluate how vividly and positively you described your visualization experience.

- **Criteria**:
    - **Detail**: Did you include vivid details about your visualization?
    - **Positivity**: Did you convey a positive and supportive audience reaction?
    - **Confidence**: Did you reflect an increase in confidence from your visualization?
- **Self-Evaluation Template**:
    - Detail: _____
    - Positivity: _____
    - Confidence: _____

Notes and Reflection

Document your visualization experience, noting any feelings of confidence or empowerment. Reflect on how visualization can positively impact your mindset and performance in speaking situations.

Reflection Questions

- **Confidence Boost**: How did the visualization exercise affect your confidence levels?

- **Mental Preparation**: Did the detailed visualization help you feel more prepared for your upcoming speaking opportunity?

- **Positive Impact**: How did imagining positive audience reactions and feedback influence your mindset?

LISA KLEIMAN

REFINE YOUR SKILLS

LISA KLEIMAN

DAY 15

Reflection and Continued Growth

Challenge

Great job! You are halfway through this program. Use this day to reflect on your journey.

Over the past two weeks, you have learned and practiced various techniques to build confidence in public speaking. Reflecting on your journey allows you to acknowledge your progress, reinforce positive changes, and set new goals for the program's second half.

Reflect on your journey halfway through the program, celebrating your progress and identifying areas for continued growth. Reflection helps solidify your achievements and sets the stage for ongoing improvement.

Exercises

Journal Your Experience

Journal about your experience overcoming your fear of public speaking. Celebrate your achievements and identify areas you still want to work on.

- **Prompts**:
    1. How did you feel during your first speech compared to now?
    2. What specific moments of progress stand out to you?

3. What positive feedback have you received, and how did it make you feel?
4. What areas do you still want to improve?

- **Example**: "When I started this program, I was extremely nervous and often stumbled over my words. I feel more confident and have received positive feedback from my colleagues about my clear delivery. I still want to reduce filler words and improve my pacing."

Speaking Exercise: Reflection Speech

Record a speech reflecting on your journey so far. Highlight your progress, achievements, and areas you still want to improve.

- **Example**: "Over the past two weeks, I have grown significantly in my public speaking skills. My confidence has improved, and I no longer feel as anxious before speaking. I have learned to engage my audience better and have received positive feedback on my clarity and body language. However, I still face challenges managing my pacing and avoiding filler words."

How to Review the Recording

When reviewing your recording, assess how you reflect on your progress and areas for improvement.

- **Criteria**:
  - **Clarity**: Did you clearly articulate your progress and achievements?
  - **Self-Awareness**: Did you honestly identify areas where you still need improvement?
  - **Goals**: Did you set realistic and specific goals for continued growth?

- **Self-Evaluation Template**:
    - Clarity: _____
    - Self-Awareness: _____
    - Goals: _____

Notes and Reflection

Consider where you started at the beginning of this 30-day plan and where you are now. How have your speaking skills improved? Consider specific growth areas, such as clarity, confidence, and body language. What improvements have you noticed in these areas? Reflect on any challenges you encountered, both internal and external. Commit to ongoing practice and learning to continue growing as a confident speaker.

Reflection Questions

- **Progress**: How have your speaking skills improved since the start of this program?

- **Achievements**: What specific achievements are you proud of?

- **Challenges**: What challenges did you face, and how did you overcome them?

- **Continued Growth**: What areas do you still want to work on, and how will you approach these challenges?

LISA KLEIMAN

DAY 16

Practice Power Posing

Challenge

Having developed relaxation techniques, positive affirmations, and visualization skills, you can now incorporate physical techniques to enhance your confidence further. Power posing builds on these mental preparations by using body language to reinforce confidence.

Use power-posing techniques to boost confidence and reduce stress before speaking. Power posing can help you adopt a more assertive and confident stance, positively affecting your mindset and performance.

Exercises

Experiment with Power Poses

Experiment with power poses for two minutes, both standing and sitting.

- **Standing Power Pose**: Stand with your feet shoulder-width apart, hands on hips or arms stretched overhead, and head held high. Hold this pose for two minutes.
- **Sitting Power Pose**: Sit with your back straight, feet flat on the floor, hands behind your head with elbows out, or arms stretched wide on the chair's armrests. Hold this pose for two minutes.

- **Example**: Stand with your feet shoulder-width apart, hands on hips, and head held high. Sit with your back straight, hands behind your head, and elbows out wide.

Notice Changes

Notice any changes in your posture, mood, or energy levels after practicing power poses.

- **Example**: Observe if you feel more confident, assertive, or energized after holding a power pose.

Daily Use

Use the power pose throughout your day when communicating with others. Incorporate power poses into your daily routine to build a habit of confident body language.

- **Example**: To boost your confidence, hold a power pose for a couple of minutes before a meeting or presentation.

Speaking Exercise: Power Pose Speech

Record a speech where you describe your experience with power posing and how it affected your confidence and performance.

- **Example**: "After practicing power poses, I felt more assertive and confident during my presentation. I noticed my posture was more open and made better eye contact with my audience."

Optional Speaking Exercise (Solo)

Stand or sit in front of a mirror and practice delivering a short speech while maintaining a power pose. Focus on maintaining a confident posture throughout your speech.

- **Example**: Stand with your hands on your hips and give a brief speech about a topic you are passionate about, maintaining the power pose throughout.

How to Review the Recording

When reviewing your recording, evaluate how effectively you explained your experience with power posing and its impact.

- **Criteria**:
    - **Clarity**: Did you clearly describe the power poses and how you performed them?
    - **Impact**: Did you effectively convey how power posing influenced your confidence and performance?
    - **Engagement**: Did you engage the audience with your insights and reflections?
- **Self-Evaluation Template**:
    - Clarity: _____
    - Impact: _____
    - Engagement: _____

Notes and Reflection

Document your experience practicing power posing, noting any changes in your confidence and stress levels. Reflect on how adopting confident body language can positively influence your public speaking.

Reflection Questions

- **Confidence Changes**: How did power posing affect your confidence levels before and during your speech?

- **Physical Sensations**: Did you notice any physical changes, such as improved posture or reduced stress?

- **Performance Impact**: How did power posing influence your overall performance and audience engagement?

DAY 17

Mastering Vocal Variety

Challenge

After building confidence through relaxation, visualization, and power posing, mastering vocal variety will further enhance your delivery skills. By learning to modulate your voice, you can make your speeches more dynamic and engaging.

Enhance your public speaking by mastering vocal variety to keep your audience engaged and convey your message effectively. Vocal variety involves changing your pitch, pace, volume, and tone to add interest and emphasize key points.

Exercises

Practice Pitch Variation

Practice varying your pitch by reading a passage out loud and intentionally changing the pitch of your voice at different points.

- **Example**: Read a paragraph from a book, varying your pitch to emphasize different emotions or ideas. Start with a high pitch for excitement and lower it for serious points.

Experiment with Pace

Practice changing your speaking pace by reading a passage at different speeds.

> **Example**: Read a paragraph slowly to convey importance, then speed up to show excitement or urgency.

Adjust Volume

Practice modulating your volume to add emphasis to certain points.

> **Example**: Read a sentence, starting softly and gradually increasing your volume to reach an important point.

Speaking Exercise: Vocal Variety Speech

Record a speech where you intentionally use vocal variety to make your message more engaging. Focus on varying your pitch, pace, and volume.

> **Example**: Give a short speech about a recent event, using a higher pitch to express excitement, slowing down your pace for key points, and raising your volume for emphasis.

Optional Speaking Exercise (Solo)

Stand before a mirror and practice delivering a short speech, focusing on using vocal variety throughout.

> **Example**: Discuss your favorite hobby, varying your pitch, pace, and volume to keep the speech lively and engaging.

How to Review the Recording

When reviewing your recording, evaluate how effectively you used vocal variety to enhance your speech.

> - **Criteria**:

- **Pitch**: Did you effectively use pitch variation to convey different emotions?
    - **Pace**: Did you vary your speaking speed to highlight key points?
    - **Volume**: Did you modulate your volume to add emphasis and maintain interest?
- **Self-Evaluation Template**:
    - Pitch: _____
    - Pace: _____
    - Volume: _____

Notes and Reflection

Document your experience practicing vocal variety, noting changes in audience engagement and overall delivery. Reflect on how using vocal variety can enhance your public speaking skills.

Reflection Questions

- **Engagement**: How did using vocal variety affect your audience's engagement?

- **Emphasis**: Which aspects of vocal variety (pitch, pace, volume) most effectively emphasized your points?

- **Improvement**: How can you continue to develop your vocal variety skills to improve your public speaking?

LISA KLEIMAN

DAY 18

Use Body Language Effectively

Challenge

Having developed a confident mindset and vocal variety, the next step is to align your body language with your verbal message. Effective body language can reinforce your words, making your delivery more compelling and credible.

Improve your public speaking by using body language effectively to complement your words and convey confidence. Body language includes gestures, facial expressions, and movements that can enhance your message.

Exercises

Practice Gestures

Practice using gestures to emphasize points in your speech. Use open and expansive gestures to convey confidence.

- **Example**: Use hand movements to illustrate size or direction, such as spreading your arms wide to show something large or pointing to indicate a specific item.

Facial Expressions

Practice varying your facial expressions to match the emotions of your speech.

- **Example**: Smile when discussing positive experiences and show concern or seriousness when discussing challenges.

Movement

Practice moving around the speaking area to engage different parts of your audience and emphasize your points.

- **Example**: Take a step forward when making a strong point, or move to the side to transition between topics.

Speaking Exercise: Body Language Speech

Record a speech where you intentionally use gestures, facial expressions, and movement to enhance your message.

- **Example**: Discuss a memorable experience, using gestures to illustrate your story, facial expressions to convey emotions, and movement to keep the audience engaged.

Optional Speaking Exercise (Solo)

Stand in front of a mirror and practice delivering a short speech, focusing on using effective body language throughout.

- **Example**: Discuss a recent project using gestures to highlight key points, facial expressions to show enthusiasm, and movement to engage your imaginary audience.

How to Review the Recording

When reviewing your recording, evaluate how effectively you used body language to enhance your speech.

- **Criteria**:

- **Gestures**: Did you use appropriate gestures to emphasize your points?
- **Facial Expressions**: Did your facial expressions match the emotions of your speech?
- **Movement**: Did you use movement to engage the audience and transition between points?

- **Self-Evaluation Template**:
  - Gestures: _____
  - Facial Expressions: _____
  - Movement: _____

Notes and Reflection

Document your experience practicing effective body language, noting any changes in audience engagement and overall delivery. Reflect on how using body language can enhance your public speaking skills.

Reflection Questions

- **Engagement**: How did using body language affect your audience's engagement?

- **Emphasis**: Which aspects of body language (gestures, facial expressions, movement) most effectively emphasized your points?

- **Improvement**: How can you continue to develop your body language skills to improve your public speaking?

LISA KLEIMAN

DAY 19

Practice Vocal Warm-ups

Challenge

Having worked on relaxation, visualization, and body language, focusing on vocal warm-ups ensures your voice is as prepared as your mind and body. This holistic approach to preparation enhances every aspect of your public speaking performance.

Integrate vocal warm-up exercises into your pre-speaking routine to improve vocal clarity, projection, and confidence. Effective vocal warm-ups can help you prepare your voice for speaking, reduce tension, and enhance your overall delivery.

Exercises

Humming

Take a deep breath through your nose, then exhale slowly while humming steadily. Focus on maintaining the consistency of the sound as you hum up and down your vocal range, from your lowest comfortable pitch to your highest. Repeat this humming exercise for 1-2 minutes to help calm your nerves.

- **Example**: "Hmmm" up and down your vocal range, ensuring a steady and consistent hum.

Tongue Twisters

Choose challenging tongue twisters, such as "Peter Piper Picked a Peck of Pickled Peppers" and "She Sells Seashells by the Seashore." Repeat each tongue twister slowly and clearly, concentrating on articulating each syllable accurately. Gradually increase your speed as you become more comfortable, repeating each tongue twister 3-5 times.

Exaggerated Pronunciation

Exaggerate pronouncing the vowels to relax facial muscles and enhance vocal resonance. Vocalize the vowels "A, E, I, O, U" while maximizing your facial expressions, repeating for 1-2 minutes.

- **Example**: Pronounce "A, E, I, O, U" with exaggerated mouth movements and facial expressions, focusing on clear and resonant sounds.

Vocal Stretches

Stand up straight, stretch your arms above your head, and take a deep breath. Exhale with a long, exaggerated sigh, allowing your voice to slide smoothly as you lower your arms. Vary the pitch and intensity of the sighing motion each time, focusing on releasing tension and warming up vocal muscles for 1-2 minutes.

- **Example**: Stretch and sigh, varying your pitch from high to low, focusing on a smooth and relaxed vocal transition.

Speaking Exercise: Warm-up Routine Speech

Record a short speech where you guide yourself (and potentially others) through your vocal warm-up routine. Focus on maintaining vocal clarity and projection throughout the speech.

- **Example**: "First, we'll start humming to warm our vocal cords. Then, we'll move on to tongue twisters like 'She sells seashells by the seashore.' Next, we'll exaggerate vowel sounds with 'A, E, I, O, U.' Finally, we'll do some vocal stretches by sighing with varied pitch."

How to Review the Recording

When reviewing your recording, assess how effectively you guided through the vocal warm-up routine and maintained clarity and projection.

- **Criteria**:
    - **Clarity**: Did you clearly explain each step of the vocal warm-up routine?
    - **Projection**: Did you maintain good vocal projection throughout the speech?
    - **Engagement**: Did you keep the routine engaging and easy to follow?
- **Self-Evaluation Template**:
    - Clarity: _____
    - Projection: _____
    - Engagement: _____

Notes and Reflection

Document your experience practicing vocal warm-ups, noting any vocal clarity or confidence improvements. Reflect on how incorporating these exercises can enhance your overall speaking performance.

Reflection Questions

- **Vocal Improvements**: How did the vocal warm-ups affect your vocal clarity and projection?

- **Confidence Boost**: Did practicing these exercises boost your confidence before speaking?

- **Routine Effectiveness**: How effective was the warm-up routine in preparing your voice for speaking engagements?

DAY 20

Develop Active Listening Skills

Challenge

Effective communication is not just about speaking; it's also about listening attentively to others. Active listening improves connections with your audience and enhances your ability to articulate ideas and respond effectively.

By developing active listening skills, you can better understand your audience's needs and respond more thoughtfully. This challenge builds on your confidence and delivery skills by emphasizing the importance of engaging with your audience.

Exercises

Practice Active Listening

Practice active listening during conversations, meetings, or presentations by focusing fully on the speaker. Use nonverbal cues such as nodding, maintaining eye contact, and providing verbal affirmations to demonstrate your engagement.

- **Example**: During a meeting, make a conscious effort to maintain eye contact with the speaker, nod in agreement, and say things like, "I see," or "That's interesting."

Paraphrasing and Summarizing

Practice paraphrasing or summarizing the speaker's key points to ensure understanding and demonstrate active listening.

- **Example**: After someone explains a concept, respond with, "So what you're saying is..." followed by a summary of their main points.

Speaking Exercise: Active Listening Speech

Record a speech where you explain the importance of active listening and share tips on practicing it effectively.

- **Example**: "Active listening is crucial for effective communication. It involves fully focusing on the speaker, using nonverbal cues, and paraphrasing their points to ensure understanding. For instance, in a conversation, you can maintain eye contact, a nod to show engagement, and summarize their message to confirm you understood correctly."

How to Review the Recording

When reviewing your recording, assess how clearly you explained the concept of active listening and provided practical tips.

- **Criteria**:
    - **Clarity**: Did you clearly explain the importance of active listening?
    - **Practicality**: Did you provide practical and actionable tips for practicing active listening?
    - **Engagement**: Did you engage the audience with your examples and explanations?
- **Self-Evaluation Template**:
    - Clarity: _____
    - Practicality: _____

- Engagement: _____

Notes and Reflection

Write down your reflections, noting any insights or observations that stand out to you. Be honest with yourself about what worked well and areas for improvement. Consider the following questions:

- **Confidence and Engagement**: Did you feel more confident, engaged, or connected with your audience?

- **Communication Effectiveness**: How did actively listening during these interactions affect your communication effectiveness?

- **Understanding and Articulation**: Did paraphrasing and summarizing help deepen your understanding of the content and improve your ability to articulate ideas?

- **Connections**: Did demonstrating genuine interest and engagement enhance your connections with colleagues, clients, or audiences?

LISA KLEIMAN

DAY 21

Speak for Emphasis

Challenge

After mastering vocal variety and effective body language, focusing on speaking for emphasis will refine your delivery. This day builds on the foundation of confidence and vocal control by teaching you how to strategically use pauses, movements, and pacing to highlight key points and maintain audience interest.

Initiating and maintaining engagement when speaking involves navigating nuances such as pacing, body language, and tone. Embrace moments of silence when speaking to allow for reflection, emphasis, and audience engagement.

Exercises
Pausing

Intentionally pause for about three seconds at key moments when speaking to emphasize important points or allow for audience reflection. Use silence to manage pacing and create anticipation in your delivery. Practice maintaining composure and confidence during moments of silence.

- **Why and How**: Pausing gives your audience time to absorb your message, adding weight to your words. It also demonstrates your control and confidence as a speaker.

- **Example**: "We have achieved remarkable results this quarter... (pause for three seconds)... results that will propel our company to new heights."

Physical Movement

Use purposeful body language to enhance your message. Step forward or lean in when making a crucial point to convey confidence and conviction. Then, step back to signal openness and receptivity to feedback.

- **Why and How**: Physical movement can help you underscore important points and engage your audience visually. Moving with purpose shows confidence and helps to maintain a dynamic presence.
- **Example**: "Our team has worked tirelessly to meet project deadlines. (Pause and step forward) I'm proud to say that our dedication has exceeded client expectations. (Step back)"

Slowing Down Speech

Avoid rushing through your speech by consciously slowing down your pace. This will allow your audience to comprehend your message fully and enhance clarity and understanding.

- **Why and How**: Slowing down your speech helps ensure that your audience can follow along and grasp the importance of your message. It also allows you to articulate your points more clearly and thoughtfully.
- **Example**: "We need to address these challenges... (slowly) step by step, with careful planning and execution."

Using Tone for Emphasis

Vary your tone to emphasize key points, convey emotions, and keep your audience engaged. Practice raising your tone for excitement and lowering it for seriousness.

- **Why and How**: Tone variation keeps your speech dynamic and helps convey the emotional weight of your message. It can signal to your audience when something is particularly important or exciting.
- **Example**: "This new initiative will revolutionize our industry (raise tone)... but only if we commit to it fully (lower tone)."

Speaking Exercise: Emphasis Speech

Record a speech where you practice using pauses, physical movement, slowed speech, and tone variation for emphasis. Focus on how these techniques enhance your delivery and audience engagement.

- **Example**: "Today, I want to discuss our strategy for the next quarter. (Pause) We have seen significant growth... (step forward), and it's just the beginning. (Pause and slow down) Each step we take must be deliberate and well-planned. (Vary tone) Together, we can achieve our goals."

How to Review the Recording

When reviewing your recording, evaluate how effectively you used pauses, physical movement, slowed speech, and tone variation to enhance your speech.

- **Criteria**:
    - **Pauses**: Did you use pauses effectively to emphasize key points and allow for audience reflection?

- **Movement**: Did your physical movements enhance your message and maintain audience engagement?
- **Pacing**: Did you maintain a clear and understandable pace throughout your speech?
- **Tone**: Did you use tone variation to emphasize key points and convey emotions?
- **Self-Evaluation Template**:
  - Pauses: _____
  - Movement: _____
  - Pacing: _____
  - Tone: _____

Notes and Reflection

Reflect on how well you managed to maintain composure during pauses, the effectiveness of your physical movements in emphasizing points, and the clarity of your message at a slower pace. Consider the following questions:

Reflection Questions

- **Composure During Pauses**: How did you feel during the pauses? Were you able to stay calm, or did you feel anxious?

- **Effectiveness of Movements**: What physical movements did you use to emphasize your points, and how effective do you think they were?

- **Clarity and Engagement**: When speaking slower, was your message clearer, and did you notice any changes in your audience's engagement?

INTEGRATION AND MASTERY

LISA KLEIMAN

DAY 22

Reflection and Continued Growth

Challenge

As you begin your final week of the 30-day speaking challenge, reflect on your journey, celebrate your progress, and set goals for continued growth. This day focuses on consolidating your learning and preparing for the final week of the 30-day speaking challenge.

This week will focus on enhancing the breadth of your speaking skills, including storytelling, persuasive pitches, and more.

Exercises

Reflection and Goal Setting

Take some time to reflect on your journey so far. Celebrate your progress and identify areas you still want to improve. Set specific goals for this final week.

- **Example**: "I have become more confident and clearer in my speech delivery. This week, I want to focus on effectively enhancing my storytelling skills and using pauses and body language."

Speaking Exercise: Reflection Speech

Option with Others:

Share your reflections and goals with a friend, family member, or colleague. Discuss your progress and areas for improvement.

- **Example**: "I've noticed significant improvements in my clarity and confidence. This week, I aim to focus on storytelling and better use of body language. What are your thoughts on my progress so far?"

Option Alone:

Record a speech reflecting on your journey so far. Highlight your progress, achievements, and areas you still want to improve.

- **Example**: "Throughout this challenge, I've seen growth in my confidence and clarity. I plan to enhance my storytelling and body language skills this week to become a more engaging speaker."

How to Review the Recording

When reviewing your recording, evaluate how well you articulated your progress, challenges, and goals.

- **Criteria**:
    - **Clarity**: Did you clearly articulate your progress and goals?
    - **Confidence**: Did you speak confidently about your achievements and areas for improvement?
    - **Engagement**: Did you engage your listener (or yourself) with your reflections?
- **Self-Evaluation Template**:
    - Clarity: _____
    - Confidence: _____
    - Engagement: _____

Notes and Reflection

Reflect on your progress so far. Consider the following questions:

Reflection Questions

- **Progress and Achievements**: What improvements have you noticed in your speaking skills? What achievements are you most proud of?

- **Challenges and Areas for Improvement**: What challenges have you faced, and how have you addressed them? What areas do you still want to work on?

- **Goals for Final Week**: What specific goals will you set for the final week of this challenge, and how will you work towards achieving them?

LISA KLEIMAN

DAY 23

Practice Impromptu Speaking

Practice thinking on your feet and responding confidently to unexpected speaking situations. Impromptu speaking builds adaptability, quick thinking, and coherent expression—important skills for handling unexpected speaking situations.

Impromptu speaking combines the confidence and clarity you've developed so far with the ability to think quickly and articulate your thoughts under pressure. This skill is crucial for real-world situations where preparation time is limited.

Exercises

Choose a Topic

Choose a random topic or question or have someone suggest a topic. Take a moment to gather your thoughts and organize your ideas.

- **Example**: Have a friend give you a random topic like "the benefits of a plant-based diet." Take a moment to gather your thoughts and organize your ideas.

Speak on It

Review the two impromptu speaking methods below and then practice speaking about your topic for one to two minutes using one of the methods (P.E.P. or P.R.E.P.). Focus on organizing your thoughts quickly and speaking clearly and confidently.

Impromptu Speaking Methods

P.E.P. (Point, Example, Point)

Start by stating your main point or argument. Provide an example or anecdote to illustrate your point. Conclude by restating your main point and reinforcing its significance.

- **Example**:
    - **Topic**: The Importance of Setting Goals
    - **Point**: Setting goals is crucial for personal and professional success.
    - **Example**: When I set a goal to run a marathon, it gave me direction and motivation to train consistently.
    - **Point**: Ultimately, setting goals helps us stay focused, motivated, and accountable.

P.R.E.P. (Point, Reason, Example, Point)

Start by stating your main point or argument. Provide a reason or rationale to support your point. Share an example or anecdote to illustrate your reasoning. Conclude by restating your main point and reinforcing its significance.

- **Example**:
    - **Topic**: The Benefits of Regular Exercise
    - **Point**: Regular exercise is essential for maintaining overall health and well-being.
    - **Reason**: Research has shown that exercise improves cardiovascular health, strengthens muscles, and boosts mood.

- **Example**: For instance, I experienced significant improvements in my energy levels and mental clarity when I started exercising regularly.
- **Point**: Incorporating regular exercise into our routines can lead to a happier, healthier lifestyle.

Speaking Exercise: Impromptu Speaking

Record yourself speaking on a random topic (it could be the same as the one you used to practice) for one to two minutes using one of the methods (P.E.P. or P.R.E.P.). Focus on organizing your thoughts quickly and speaking clearly and confidently.

How to Review the Recording

When reviewing your recording, evaluate how well you organized your thoughts, maintained coherence and clarity, and delivered your message under pressure.

- **Criteria**:
  - **Organization**: Did you structure your thoughts clearly and logically?
  - **Clarity**: Were you able to express your ideas clearly and effectively?
  - **Confidence**: Did you speak confidently and handle the impromptu nature of the task well?
- **Self-Evaluation Template**:
  - Organization: _____
  - Clarity: _____
  - Confidence: _____

Notes and Reflection

Document your experience practicing impromptu speaking, noting any challenges or successes you encountered. Reflect on the following questions:

Reflection Questions

- **Structure and Organization**: How well did you structure your thoughts? Could you maintain coherence and clarity under pressure?
- **Adaptability**: How comfortable did you feel thinking on your feet and speaking without preparation?
- **Confidence and Versatility**: How did practicing this skill increase your confidence and versatility as a speaker?

DAY 24

Speak Persuasively

Challenge

Enhance your public speaking skills by delivering concise and persuasive messages within a short time frame, such as an elevator pitch. Communicate a clear and compelling argument that convinces your audience to take a specific action.

Building on your confidence, clarity, and impromptu speaking skills, this challenge focuses on crafting and delivering persuasive messages. It helps you refine your ability to present arguments succinctly and compellingly, a crucial skill for influencing and motivating your audience.

Exercises

Outline Your Pitch

Choose a topic you feel strongly about and prepare a short persuasive speech advocating for your position. Focus on building credibility, presenting compelling evidence, and making a strong call to action.

- **Example**: Choose a topic like advocating for renewable energy. Follow this template:

Introduction

Start with a compelling question, statistic, or anecdote. Clearly state your viewpoint or decision.

- **Example**:
    - **Attention Grabber**: "Did you know that renewable energy could save the average household $200 a year?"
    - **Statement of Purpose**: "We need to invest more in renewable energy sources."

Body

Present your first argument using evidence or personal examples. Introduce your second argument, connecting emotionally with the listener. Present a final compelling argument addressing concerns.

- **Example**:
    - **Main Point 1**: "Renewable energy reduces greenhouse gas emissions."
    - **Main Point 2**: "It also creates jobs in our community."
    - **Main Point 3**: "Moreover, renewable energy sources like wind and solar are becoming more cost-effective."

Conclusion

Recap the main arguments. Encourage action or further discussion.

- **Example**:
    - **Summary of Key Points**: "To sum up, renewable energy benefits the environment, the economy, and our future."
    - **Call to Action**: "Let's support policies that promote renewable energy and make a positive impact together."

Speaking Exercise: Persuasive Speech

Record a speech where you deliver your outlined persuasive message. Focus on building credibility, presenting compelling evidence, and making a strong call to action.

- **Example**: "Today, I want to talk about the importance of renewable energy. Did you know that renewable energy could save the average household $200 a year? We need to invest more in renewable energy sources. Renewable energy reduces greenhouse gas emissions, creates jobs in our community, and is becoming more cost-effective. To sum up, renewable energy benefits the environment, the economy, and our future. Let's support policies that promote renewable energy and make a positive impact together."

How to Review the Recording

When reviewing your recording, evaluate how effectively you conveyed your message, built credibility, and made a compelling call to action.

- **Criteria**:
    - **Clarity**: Did you clearly articulate your points and arguments?
    - **Credibility**: Did you provide compelling evidence or examples to support your arguments?
    - **Call to Action**: Was your call to action clear and persuasive?
- **Self-Evaluation Template**:
    - Clarity: _____
    - Credibility: _____
    - Call to Action: _____

Notes and Reflection

Evaluate the effectiveness of your persuasive message. Consider the following questions:

Reflection Questions

- **Message Conveyance**: Did you effectively convey your message?

- **Audience Response**: How did your audience respond?

- **Refinement**: How can you refine your argument to make it more convincing?

DAY 25

Network and Converse

Challenge

This challenge builds on the active listening skills and confidence you've developed so far. Networking and conversing with new people will help you apply these skills in real-world scenarios, enhancing your ability to connect and communicate effectively.

Engage in at least two conversations with strangers or acquaintances, focusing on active listening and asking open-ended questions to keep the conversation flowing smoothly.

Exercises

Initiate Conversations

Approach two people (colleagues, friends of friends, or strangers in a social setting). Initiate a conversation with a friendly greeting and introduce yourself.

- **Example**: Approach a colleague you don't know well at work, a friend of a friend at a social gathering, and a stranger at a community event. Start with a friendly greeting and introduce yourself.

Ask Open-Ended Questions

Ask open-ended questions such as, "What brings you here today?" or "What projects are you currently working on?" or "What's been keeping you busy lately?"

Practice Active Listening

Maintain eye contact, nod, and ask follow-up questions based on their responses, like "Can you tell me more about that?" or "How did you get involved in that project?". Aim to keep the conversation going for at least five minutes.

Speaking Exercise: Networking Practice

Record a summary speech in which you share your experience initiating and engaging in conversations with new people. Reflect on what strategies helped you engage effectively.

How to Review the Recording

When reviewing your recording, evaluate how well you initiated conversations, asked open-ended questions, and practiced active listening.

- **Criteria**:
    - **Initiation**: How smoothly did you initiate the conversation?
    - **Open-Ended Questions**: Did you ask questions that encouraged detailed responses?
    - **Active Listening**: Did you demonstrate active listening through eye contact, nodding, and follow-up questions?
- **Self-Evaluation Template**:
    - Initiation: _____
    - Open-Ended Questions: _____
    - Active Listening: _____

Notes and Reflection

Note any improvement in your conversational skills. Consider the following questions:

Reflection Questions

- **Challenges**: What did you find challenging about initiating and maintaining conversations?

- **Engagement Strategies**: What strategies helped you engage effectively?

- **Skills Improvement**: How did this exercise help improve your networking and conversational skills?

LISA KLEIMAN

DAY 26

Craft and Deliver Compelling Stories

Challenge

This challenge leverages the confidence and clarity you've built so far, adding depth and engagement through storytelling, a key element of effective public speaking.

Exercises

Reflect and Jot Down Key Points

Craft and deliver compelling stories that resonate with your audience. Choose a memorable experience from your life that you feel comfortable sharing. This could be a funny incident, a lesson learned, or a moment of triumph. Reflect on your chosen story and jot down key points or details you want to include.

- **Example**: If your story is about a lesson learned from a failed project, jot down the project's goal, the mistake made, the consequences, and the lesson learned.

Practice Aloud

Practice telling your story aloud, focusing on clarity, pacing, and expression. Use the template below as your guide. Once confident, share your story with colleagues, friends, or loved ones.

- **Example**: Practice telling your story about a funny travel experience, focusing on how you describe the setting, the mishap, and the humorous outcome.

Storytelling Guide

Setting the Scene

Begin by painting a vivid picture of the setting. Describe the location, time, and environment to draw your audience into the story.

- **Example**: "It was a sunny afternoon in a quaint Spanish village, with cobblestone streets and colorful buildings lining the narrow alleys."

Introducing Characters

Introduce the main characters involved in your story. Provide brief descriptions to help your audience visualize them.

- **Example**: "I was traveling with my friend, Maria, who has an adventurous spirit and a knack for finding hidden gems."

Building Tension

Build tension by describing the challenge or conflict you faced. Use detailed descriptions to convey the emotions and stakes involved.

- **Example**: "As we wandered the village, we realized we were hopelessly lost. The narrow streets looked identical, and our map was no help."

Climax and Resolution

Narrate the climax of your story—the turning point where the main event or realization occurs. Then, describe how the situation was resolved.

- **Example**: "Just when we were about to give up, we heard the distant sound of music. Following the melody, we stumbled upon a lively local festival with dancing, food, and laughter. It was the highlight of our trip, turning a moment of panic into an unforgettable experience."

Reflecting on the Lesson

Conclude your story by reflecting on the lesson learned or the significance of the experience. Relate it to a broader theme or message.

- **Example**: "This experience taught me that sometimes getting lost can lead to the most unexpected and delightful adventures. It reminded me to embrace the journey, no matter how uncertain it may seem."

Speaking Exercise: Storytelling
Option with Others:

Share your story with a friend, family member, or colleague. Ask for feedback on how engaging and clear your storytelling was.

- **Example**: "I'd like to tell you about my experience traveling in Spain. Please let me know your thoughts on my storytelling and if it was engaging."

Option Alone:

Record a speech where you tell your story compellingly and engagingly, focusing on setting the scene, building tension, and delivering a satisfying conclusion.

- **Example**: "During my trip to Spain, I explored a small village. I got lost, but in the process, I stumbled upon a local festival that turned out to be the highlight of my trip."

How to Review the Recording

When reviewing your recording, evaluate how effectively you set the scene, introduced characters, built tension, and delivered the climax and resolution.

- **Criteria**:
    - **Setting**: Did you paint a vivid picture of the setting?
    - **Characters**: Did you introduce the characters in a way that helped the audience visualize them?
    - **Tension**: Did you build tension effectively to keep the audience engaged?
    - **Climax and Resolution**: Did you narrate the climax and resolution clearly and compellingly?
- **Self-Evaluation Template**:
    - Setting: _____
    - Characters: _____
    - Tension: _____
    - Climax and Resolution: _____

Notes and Reflection

Reflect on your experience of sharing a personal story. Consider the following questions:

Reflection Questions

- **Emotional Experience**: How did you feel during the storytelling process? What emotions did you experience?

- **Audience Response**: How did your audience respond to your story, and what feedback did you receive?

- **Insights Gained**: What insights did you gain about the power of personal storytelling, and how can you use this experience to build confidence in your public speaking?

LISA KLEIMAN

DAY 27

Develop Active Listening Skills

Challenge

Effective communication is not just about speaking; it's also about listening attentively to others. Active listening improves connections with your audience and your ability to articulate ideas and respond effectively.

Building on your confidence, clarity, and storytelling skills, this challenge emphasizes the importance of active listening. It helps you become a more effective communicator by enhancing your ability to understand and respond to others.

Exercises

Practice Active Listening

Practice active listening during conversations, meetings, or presentations by focusing fully on the speaker. Use nonverbal cues such as nodding, maintaining eye contact, and providing verbal affirmations to demonstrate your engagement.

- **Example**: During a team meeting, focus on the speaker, nod to show understanding, maintain eye contact, and say things like "I see," or "That makes sense."

Paraphrasing and Summarizing

Practice paraphrasing or summarizing the speaker's key points to ensure understanding and demonstrate active listening.

- **Example**: After listening to a colleague's update, you might say, "So, what you're saying is that we need to adjust our timeline to meet the new project deadlines?"

Speaking Exercise: Active Listening Speech

Engage in a conversation with a friend, family member, or colleague. After the conversation, record a speech explaining the importance of active listening and sharing tips on practicing it effectively.

- **Example**: "In my conversation with [Friend's Name], I practiced active listening by maintaining eye contact and summarizing their key points. This helped me understand their perspective better and made the conversation more engaging."

How to Review the Recording

When reviewing your recording, evaluate how well you explained the importance of active listening and shared practical tips.

- **Criteria**:
    - **Clarity**: Did you clearly explain the concept and importance of active listening?
    - **Engagement**: Did you share practical and engaging tips for practicing active listening?
    - **Reflection**: Did you reflect effectively on your active listening practices?
- **Self-Evaluation Template**:
    - Clarity: _____

- Engagement: _____
- Reflection: _____

Notes and Reflection

Write down your reflections, noting any insights or observations that stand out to you. Consider the following questions:

Reflection Questions

- **Confidence and Engagement**: Did you feel more confident, engaged, or connected with your audience while practicing active listening?

- **Effectiveness**: How did actively listening during these interactions affect your communication effectiveness?

- **Understanding and Articulation**: Did paraphrasing and summarizing help deepen your understanding of the content and improve your ability to articulate ideas?

- **Connections**: Did demonstrating genuine interest and engagement enhance your connections with colleagues, clients, or audiences?

LISA KLEIMAN

DAY 28

Master Your Pitch

Challenge

Mastering the elevator pitch is crucial for professionals to convey ideas effectively. This skill isn't just for business; it's also useful for persuading in daily life. In this exercise, you will refine your pitch to engage audiences in business and personal settings.

Exercises

Choose a Specific Pitch

Select a specific idea, product, service, or personal matter to pitch with a defined objective—attracting investors, gaining new clients, persuading a spouse or friend, or generating interest or support.

- **Example**: Choose to pitch a new app designed to help users track their fitness goals.

Design Your Pitch

Design your pitch to highlight key points, focusing on capturing attention, generating curiosity, and compelling action.

- **Example**:
  - **Attention Grabber**: "Did you know that 70% of people abandon their fitness goals within the first month?"

- **Key Features**: "Our app, BFitHappy, keeps you motivated by providing personalized workout plans and progress tracking."
- **Benefits**: "Users of BFitHappy have seen a 50% increase in their adherence to fitness routines."

Record and Review

Find a quiet space free from distractions, and imagine you have only 30-60 seconds to pitch your idea. Use a smartphone or recording device to record yourself delivering the pitch, emphasizing clarity, confidence, and enthusiasm.

- **Example**: Record your pitch for BFitHappy, focusing on maintaining a confident and enthusiastic tone.

Seek Feedback

Review the recording, noting areas for improvement in tone, pace, gestures, and overall delivery. Invite a friend, family member, or colleague to listen to your pitch and provide constructive feedback.

- **Example**: Ask a friend to watch your recorded pitch and provide feedback on your delivery and clarity.

Refine and Practice

Practice your pitch as if in a real-life scenario, considering the context of persuading different audiences. Refine your pitch based on feedback and practice delivering it multiple times to enhance your confidence and persuasiveness.

- **Example**: Refine your pitch based on feedback, focusing on improving your pace and incorporating more engaging body language. Practice delivering your pitch multiple times until it feels natural.

Speaking Exercise: Real-Life Practice

Identify opportunities to deliver your pitch in a real-world setting. This could be a networking event, a meeting with potential clients, or a casual conversation with a friend or family member.

- **Identify Opportunities**: Look for opportunities to deliver your pitch in a real-world setting.
- **Real-Life Practice**: If a real-life opportunity isn't immediately available, simulate the scenario as closely as possible. Stand up, dress appropriately, and imagine the setting where you would typically give this pitch.
- **Deliver Your Pitch**: Deliver your pitch confidently, ensuring you incorporate all the feedback and improvements you've worked on. Focus on maintaining eye contact, using engaging body language, and keeping your tone persuasive and enthusiastic.
- **Example**: Imagine you are at a networking event and meet a potential investor for your startup. Your goal is to capture their interest in under a minute.
- **Template**: "Hi, my name is [Your Name], and I'm the founder of [Your Company]. Have you ever felt overwhelmed by the time it takes to manage your daily tasks? Our product, [Product Name], is designed to streamline your workflow and boost productivity by [Briefly Describe Key Features]. Studies have shown that using [Product Name] can save users up to 10 hours a week. We're currently looking for investors who share our vision of transforming the way people work. I would love to discuss how we can partner to

bring this innovative solution to more users. Could we set up a time to talk further?"

Notes and Reflection

Reflect on how your confidence and comfort level evolved throughout the session and how seeking feedback contributed to your progress. Consider what actions you will take to refine and enhance your elevator pitch, integrating the lessons learned. Assess specific areas such as pacing, clarity, and emotional appeal, and outline a plan to continue improving these aspects in future practice sessions.

DAY 29

Cultivate Gratitude

Challenge

Cultivate gratitude for the opportunity to speak and share your message with others, shifting your focus from fear to appreciation.

By focusing on gratitude, you reinforce the positive aspects of your speaking journey, helping to transform fear into appreciation. This mindset shift can further boost your confidence and motivation as a speaker.

Exercises

Express Gratitude

Set aside moments throughout the day to express gratitude for the ability to communicate and connect with others through speaking. Reflect on past speaking experiences that have brought you joy or fulfillment.

- **Example**: Reflect on a time when your speech made a difference, like receiving heartfelt feedback from an audience member inspired by your words.

Positive Impact

Notice your words' positive impact on others and be grateful for the opportunity to make a difference.

- **Example**: Recall when your message helped someone gain clarity or confidence and express gratitude for that opportunity.

Speaking Exercise: Gratitude Speech

Record a speech where you express gratitude for your speaking journey. Highlight moments of joy, fulfillment, and positive impact you have experienced through speaking.

- **Example**: "I am grateful for the opportunity to speak and share my message. One memorable moment was when I spoke at a community event, and a young person told me how my words inspired them to pursue their dreams. These experiences remind me of the power of communication and the positive impact we can have on others."

How to Review the Recording

When reviewing your recording, evaluate how sincerely you expressed gratitude and highlighted positive experiences.

- **Criteria**:
    - **Sincerity**: Did you convey genuine gratitude in your speech?
    - **Highlighting Positive Experiences**: Did you effectively highlight moments of joy, fulfillment, and positive impact?
    - **Emotional Connection**: Did your speech convey an emotional connection with your audience?
- **Self-Evaluation Template**:

- Sincerity:
- Highlighting Positive Experiences:
- Emotional Connection:

Notes and Reflection

Document your reflections on cultivating gratitude in your speaking practice. Consider the following questions:

Reflection Questions

- **Perspective Shift**: How did focusing on gratitude shift your perspective or attitude toward speaking?

- **Positive Reinforcement**: What positive impacts did you notice in your speaking journey for which you are grateful?

- **Fuel for Passion**: How can gratitude fuel your passion and motivation for sharing your message?

LISA KLEIMAN

DAY 30

Celebrate Your Growth

Challenge

You made it – you are on your last day of this 30-day challenge! Bravo!

Celebrate your progress and growth throughout the 30-day challenge, recognizing your achievements and newfound confidence as a speaker.

Celebrating your achievements reinforces positive habits and builds a sense of accomplishment. This reflection solidifies your learning and prepares you for growth beyond the challenge.

Exercises

Write a Personal Commitment

Craft a personal commitment statement outlining your dedication to ongoing practice and growth as a confident speaker. Include specific actions you will take to continue developing your skills and overcoming challenges. Write this commitment statement in the present tense to reinforce your commitment and motivation.

- **Example**: "I am committed to continuing my journey as a confident speaker by practicing regularly, seeking feedback, and participating in speaking events."

Celebrate Achievements

Celebrate your achievements, no matter how small, and acknowledge the growth and improvements you've experienced as a speaker. To mark the completion of this 30-day plan, treat yourself to a reward or special activity.

- **Example**: Celebrate by having a nice dinner, spending the day doing an activity you enjoy, or sharing your success with friends and family.

Speaking Exercise: Celebration Speech

Share your journey and accomplishments with friends, family, or colleagues. Include your commitment to ongoing practice, specific goals you want to achieve, and how you plan to stay motivated.

- **Example**: "Completing this 30-day challenge has been a significant milestone in my public speaking journey. I've become more confident and articulate in my speaking. I've learned to use pauses effectively and tell compelling stories. I am committed to practicing regularly, participating in speaking events, and seeking feedback to improve. My goal is to become a keynote speaker at industry conferences, and I will stay motivated by celebrating small victories and learning from every experience."

Notes and Reflection

Reflect on the journey you've taken over the past 30 days, noting the challenges you've overcome and the skills you've developed. Consider the following questions:

Reflection Questions

- **Improvements**: How have your speaking skills improved? Consider specific growth areas, such as clarity, confidence, and body language.
- **Strategies**: What strategies did you implement to overcome these challenges? Did you develop a consistent practice routine? Seek feedback from peers or mentors? Utilize relaxation techniques to manage nerves?
- **Effectiveness**: Which strategies were most effective for you and why?
- **Changes**: Do you notice any changes in confidence, competence, or comfort level with public speaking after completing this challenge?
- **Future Plans**: How will you continue to build upon your progress and further develop your speaking skills?

YOU DID IT!

Congratulations on completing the **Overcome Your Fear of Public Speaking** program. Over 30 days, you've dedicated yourself to confronting your fears, honing your speaking skills, and building confidence as a communicator. Through daily exercises, reflection, and practice, you've made significant strides toward overcoming the obstacles that once held you back.

As you reflect on your journey, remember to celebrate your progress and achievements, no matter how small they may seem. Each step you've taken has brought you closer to becoming the confident, articulate speaker you aspire to be.

Moving forward, apply the strategies and techniques you've learned throughout the challenge. Whether preparing for a high-stakes presentation, a job interview, or a casual conversation, draw upon the skills and mindset you've developed to approach speaking opportunities with confidence and poise.

Remember that growth is a continuous process, and there will always be opportunities for learning and improvement. Keep challenging yourself, pushing beyond your comfort zone, and embracing new speaking challenges with enthusiasm and resilience.

May your newfound confidence in public speaking open doors to new opportunities, connections, and successes in all aspects of your life. Here's to your continued growth and success as a speaker!

Lisa Kleiman

ADDITIONAL TRAINING

We trust you found value in this workbook and hope you feel more assured about your skills and have a clear path to becoming an engaging and confident speaker.

Building resilience and confidence as a public speaker is an ongoing journey. Sustain your momentum with our ongoing training options for continual growth.

See www.speaktopia.com for training options.

For any questions or assistance, contact us at

hello@speaktopia.com.

We'd love to hear from you!

Happy Speaking,

Lisa

www.ingramcontent.com/pod-product-compliance
Lightning Source LLC
Chambersburg PA
CBHW072209070526
44585CB00015B/1255